SO YOU'RE
65!

Mike Haskins & Clive Whichelow

Illustrations by Ian Baker

summersdale

SO YOU'RE 65!

Illustrations by Ian Baker

Summersdale Publishers Ltd
46 West Street
Chichester
West Sussex
PO19 1RP
UK

www.summersdale.com

Printed and bound in Poland

ISBN: 978-1-84953-726-1

Substantial discounts on bulk quantities of Summersdale books are available to corporations, professional associations and other organisations. For details contact Nicky Douglas by telephone: +44 (0) 1243 756902, fax: +44 (0) 1243 786300 or email: nicky@summersdale.com.

To.................................

From.............................

INTRODUCTION

Eek! This is the big one! You're now a pensioner (possibly – pension rules are one of the many things you can't keep up with these days). It doesn't matter that you may still be working because you now qualify for a state pension. It's official!

You will already have your bus pass and probably a national travel card, too. This is because you're so old and decrepit that you need to be ferried around everywhere like a sack of potatoes, in only a slightly grander style.

Despite this, you are as fit as a fiddle, aren't you? You may play squash regularly – we're not talking about when you sit on the sofa cushions – and you might still be running marathons rather than eating them as you did in days of yore, but...

After this, the next stop is 70! Well, actually, the next stop is 66 but that doesn't prevent people (usually younger people) from saying 'Next stop 70!', as if you're on some sort of special geriatric bus route.

But being 65 has its advantages – apart from that whopping great state pension, of course – because 65 is the new 55, and as 55 is the new 45 you will see that before long you will be a teenager again. In your mind, you always have been. All you've got to do now is convince everyone else! Happy sixty-fifth!

WHAT BEING 65 MEANS

It's ten years till you get your free TV licence (by which time everything will be online or available on subscription only)

It's just 35 years till you receive your telegram from the Queen (or possibly a text message from King William V)

WHAT BEING 65 MEANS TO OTHER CREATURES

*Giant tortoise –
all the other giant
tortoises call you 'kid'*

Gorilla – you're a silverback or, if a lady gorilla, a blue-rinse back

Komodo dragon – you remember being visited by David Attenborough when he was a slim, floppy-haired, young boy

REASONS WHY YOU MAY STILL BE WORKING

The state pension barely covers your bar bills for the week, let alone food

You need to put right all the mistakes you have made over the past forty or so years

It's easier than doing all the things your spouse wants you to sort out at home

THE PROS AND CONS OF GIVING UP WORK

PRO: You can devote all your time to your hobbies and leisure interests

CON: After a couple of hours you realise your hobbies and leisure interests are not quite as enthralling as you first thought

PRO: You can spend all day
watching daytime TV

CON: Have you seen
daytime TV?

GIVEAWAYS
THAT YOU
MIGHT BE 65

Your mobile phone
has a dial rather
than buttons

You get all misty-eyed
about trolleybuses

LEISURE PURSUITS – THE PROS AND CONS OF RAMBLING

PRO: *You can enjoy being out in the countryside*

CON: *You may be used for target practice by a farmer wanting you to get off their land*

PRO: You can wander around for the entire day as you see fit

CON: Anxious relatives keep calling out the helicopter rescue service to look for you

WORDS THAT HAVE CHANGED MEANING IN YOUR LIFETIME

POUND

THEN: A day's wages
NOW: Loose change

SPAM

THEN: Tinned meat
NOW: Unwanted email

THINGS YOU WON'T BE ABLE TO DO ANY MORE

Sing 'When I'm 64'
with any degree of
factual accuracy

Make any sudden movement without then having to book a session with a masseuse

THINGS THAT MIGHT HAPPEN THESE DAYS

People will automatically assume that you have grandchildren

You get your five-a-day fruit
and veg target confused with
your daily alcohol limit

Somebody who looks quite elderly will get up to offer you their seat on the bus

DOS AND DON'TS FOR YOUR RETIREMENT FUND

DO: Purchase an annuity that will provide a regular income for the rest of your life

DON'T: Put the entire pension fund you've built up over the years on a horse or lottery scratch cards

DO: Convert part of your fund into cash

DON'T: Convert your entire fund into cash and leave it piled up near an open window during high winds

DO: *Allow yourself the occasional treat*

DON'T: *Emulate the lifestyles of the Queen of Sheba or Elton John*

SIGNS YOUR EMPLOYER MAY WANT YOU TO RETIRE

They use phrases such as
'You're still here then?' or
'Remind me, who are
you again?'

*They encourage you
to work from home even
though you are a coal miner,
brain surgeon or air
traffic controller*

WHY BEING 65 IS LIKE BEING 18 AGAIN

No job
(if you're lucky)

No mortgage
(if you're lucky)

*If you want, you can lie
around in bed all day*

WHY BEING 65 IS NOT LIKE BEING 18 AGAIN

You can't have a lie-in because you always wake up desperately needing the toilet

*You don't have
the energy to get to
the bus stop*

THINGS
PEOPLE WILL
ASK YOU TO
CRAFTILY TRY
TO WORK OUT
YOUR AGE

'So what was rationing like?'

'Do you remember if the first record you ever bought was a 78 rpm or a wax cylinder?'

'Did you get the day off school for the coronation?'

LEISURE PURSUITS – THE PROS AND CONS OF TRACING YOUR FAMILY HISTORY

PRO: You discover close blood relatives you didn't know you had

CON: One of them is the person you've been married to for the past 30 years

PRO: You can spend many hours happily absorbed in your new hobby

CON: You will have to pay someone else to do the cleaning and gardening while you're glued to your laptop

THINGS PEOPLE WILL SEEK YOUR ADVICE ON

*How you managed to reach
65 and yet still stay looking
so young*

How you managed to reach
65 when you look as much
of a wreck as you do

*How they can avoid
ending up like you*

THINGS YOU REMEMBER THAT KIDS OF TODAY DON'T

People not being able to contact you at all times of the day or night no matter where you are

Having a phone that didn't take pictures

WHY 65 (ISH) HAS TRADITIONALLY BEEN THE AGE OF THE PENSIONER

Because if it were 55-ish the government would go broke paying the state pension

If it were 75-ish they would have no one to staff all the charity shops

THINGS YOU WILL FEEL CONFIDENT ABOUT

*You can boast that you
still have to pay for your
TV licence*

If someone you've not met before is over-cheerful and friendly, they are about to try to sell you something

You can remember when shopkeepers used to fetch your purchases for you

THE UPSIDE OF BEING 65

You can look back on a wholly virtuous life – and if you can't, you've probably got away with it all by now

Finally, at long last, you're getting something back from the government! Hooray!

If you're interested in finding out more about our books, find us on Facebook at Summersdale Publishers and follow us on Twitter at @Summersdale.

www.summersdale.com